Becca's Bike

by Justin McCory Martin
illustrated by Margeaux Lucas

SCHOLASTIC INC.

New York • Toronto • London • Auckland
Sydney • Mexico City • New Delhi • Hong Kong

ISBN 978-0-545-68601-3

12 11 10 9 8 7 6 5 4 3 2 1 14 15 16 17 18 19/0

Printed in China.

One day, Becca's mom gave her a bike.

"This belonged to me when I was your age," she said proudly. "Why don't you take it for a spin?"

How do you think Becca feels about the bike? How do you know?

The bike embarrassed Becca. It was old and dented. It had a basket and a bell that went *ring-a-ling!*

What does the sign on the tree say?

Becca saw her friend Kay. Kay had a cool bike. It was purple with pink streamers.

"What a great bike!" said Becca.

"Your bike sure is . . . interesting," said Kay.

Becca and Kay rode off together.

"This basket is so big!" said Becca.

"But it will come in handy if you ever need to carry something," said Kay.

Becca and Kay met Ben. Ben had a cool bike, too. It was orange with bright yellow flames.

"What a great bike!" said Becca.

"Your bike sure is . . . unusual," said Ben.

How are Becca's and Ben's bikes alike? How are they different?

Becca and her friends rode off together.
Ring-a-ling, ring-a-ling!

"This bell is so loud!" said Becca.

"But it'll come in handy if you ever need to get people's attention," said Ben.

The three friends rode toward the playground. They wanted to take a shortcut across the field. But there was a problem: The path was all muddy.

Why would a muddy path be a problem?

"I can't ride in that mud," said Kay. "It will mess up my bike."

"Me neither. Let's take the long way," said Ben.

But Becca did not mind getting her bike dirty.

"I'll meet you there," she said, riding off along the muddy path.

On the path, Becca saw a surprising sight. It was Sparky! Sparky was a lost dog that belonged to her neighbor, Mrs. Minden.

What do you think Becca will do next?

Becca got off her bike and walked over to Sparky. He looked really scared! She picked up the little dog and put him in the bike's basket. Then she rode to the playground.

At the playground, Becca's friends were amazed.

"You found Sparky!" said Kay.

"You're a hero!" said Ben.

Have you ever helped an animal in need?

The three friends rode to Mrs. Minden's house. Becca rang her bell all the way there. *Ring-a-ling, ring-a-ling, ring-a-ling!*

Mrs. Minden was thrilled to see her dog.

"Thanks, Becca," she said. "And thanks to your bike. It helped you rescue Sparky."

"This bike belonged to my mom," said Becca proudly. "I think I'll take it for a spin!"

How do you think Becca feels about her bike at the end of the story?

Story Prompts

Answer these questions after you have read the book.

1. Can you think of some great words to describe Becca's bike?

2. What other adventures could Becca have with her bike? Turn on your imagination and tell a story about one!

3. If you could have any bike in the world, what would it be like?